A

BiG thoughts for **Little** minds

Production

ACKNOWLEDGMENTS:
TEXT: Ivan Gouveia, based on Galatians 5, verses 22–23, the Bible.
ILLUSTRATIONS: Leilen Basan
DESIGN: Leilen Basan, M-A Mignot

ISBN: 978-1-63264-052-9

© 2015 Ivan Gouveia and Leilen Basan.

All Rights Reserved.

Published by Book Barn Publishing.

Printed in China.

Different

KINDS OF

Fruit

BASED ON GALATIANS 5, VERSES 22-23 – THE FRUITS OF THE SPIRIT

Dedicated to:

_____

From:

_____

I read once that when we live in God's light and are obedient to His Word, there are certain qualities that His Spirit will give us that will help us to live a full and happy life.

These qualities were compared to fruits that good trees would have. I thought that was a fun way to remember them.

The first fruit is love. I will always try to speak and act in a loving manner with everyone I see. When we truly live in love we prefer others' well-being above our own.

The second fruit is joy! When I live a life of gratefulness for all that I receive and get to do, I am happy all day long. True happiness comes to me when I try to make others happy.

4

The third fruit is peace. Since I believe that God will always care for me, I don't ever have to be worried or fearful. Not even at night! He will always be with me.

5

The fourth fruit is patience. I will be calm even if things don't work out right away. Things can take a little while at times, but I should trust that those who look after me know best.

The fifth fruit is kindness. I will be kind to those around me, even to those who are not so kind to me. I will go out of my way to help those who need my help in any way I can.

The sixth fruit is goodness. This doesn't mean that I will be good all the time, but I can choose to be polite, fair, and truthful in all my actions.

8

The seventh fruit is faithfulness. I will keep working hard at whatever task I set out to do. I will not give up even when it gets very hard or boring. I know that no matter what it is, God will help me to complete it.

9

The eighth fruit is gentleness.
I will treat others with respect,
especially those older than me,
and will talk to anyone I meet
in a polite and considerate
manner. Being loud and rude
is definitely not cool.

PRIVATE
PROPERTY

The ninth fruit is self-control. I will follow the rules that help me build good habits and keep me safe, even when no one is watching. I won't do things that I know are wrong.

I can assure you that if you take all these fruits and make yourself a nice, colorful, and delicious fruit shake...

...life will be much more fun, happy, and tasty! A big toast to the fruits of the spirit!

13

My big thoughts!

1 Think about good qualities or traits you would like to have? What are they?

2 Try naming the different good fruits mentioned in this book. How many can you remember?

3 Do I do my best to act in a loving way toward others? How can I improve in showing love to others?

4 Can you think of a time when you felt happy because you made someone else happy? Try making someone happy today.

5 Do you feel unsure of yourself or afraid at times? Remember to ask for God's peace of mind whenever you feel that way.

6 Isn't it difficult to be patient at times? Do you remember a time when you were rewarded with something you really wanted after waiting patiently?

Think
Think
Think

7 Imagine some scenarios or situations which could happen daily, at school or at home, where you could perform deeds of kindness.

8 Have you ever been tempted to cheat in a game or on a test? Doesn't it feel much better when you are truthful and honorable?

9 Do you ever feel like quitting when a job is difficult or if it takes a long time to complete? Try finishing your next task completely and see how great that feels!

10 Greeting people politely shows courtesy. Practice with your mom or dad how you would greet someone you haven't met before.

11 Do you sometimes feel like doing something you know you shouldn't? Talk about one of the rules in your house, and how it helps you and why it's important.

12 Do you think you could learn all these virtues and find ways to apply them in your everyday life? Think of how much happier you would be if you did!

13 Conduct an experiment. Pick a virtue listed in this book and look for ways you can put it into action in your day.

Think
Think
Think